Earth Movers

Trace Taylor

This is an excavator. An excavator digs up dirt and rocks with a bucket shovel.

This one is yellow.

This excavator is fitted with a digging bucket shovel.

 This one is orange.

Bucket shovels come in different widths and depths. The size and shape of the bucket must fit the kind of hole needed.

This one is **black**.

Some buckets are big enough to hold a small car or truck.

6 This one is orange.

Excavators are also used to tear down old buildings, break up old roads, and work in scrap metal yards. Workers just change the attachment at the end of the arm.

This one is green.

This excavator is fitted with a grapple.

8 This one is **blue**.

Grapples can have as few as 2 claws and as many as 8. Notice the teeth on the claws.

This one is **black**.

Some excavators are fitted with a jackhammer attachment. They use this to break up concrete and rocks.

This one is red.

This excavator has a broken clamshell digger.

This one is white.

The bucket shovel or grapple is attached to the arm. The arm is attached to the cab, where the driver sits.

This one is yellow.

Most excavators do not have wheels. They have tracks like an armored tank. This keeps them from getting stuck in the mud.

This one is green.

You will often see excavators filling up dump trucks.

This one is **black**.

Some dump trucks are the size of pickup trucks. Some dump trucks are bigger than houses.

This one is red.

Dump trucks are used in almost every type of construction work. They haul dirt and rocks from one place to another.

This one is white.

Tractors are also used in construction. This monster tractor can pull full trailors or big plows used to till the soil. They are also used to pull bigger diggers out of mud holes.

This one is **blue**.

A backhoe has an arm and shovel on the back and a bucket on the front. It can dig holes and carry the dirt away.

This is a wheeled bulldozer. Bulldozers are big, tough muscle tractors with scoops on the front. They can lift or move almost anything.

Floating barges, cranes, and excavators are used to deepen and clean out harbors and canals. This is called dredging. Dredging keeps the waterways deep enough for use by bigger boats.

This extreme machine is a bucket-wheel excavator. It is the largest land vehicle ever built in human history. It is more than 1 football field tall and more than 2 football fields long. It weighs more than 11,000 tons. Notice the truck and bulldozer to the right.

Truck   Bulldozer

Coal, iron, and gold are just a few of the substances harvested by this digger. This machine is used when the minerals are close to the surface. It can dig through more than 59 acres of earth a day. That's like a big shopping mall, including all the parking lots.

A landfill is a big hole dug in the earth where trash gets dumped. These huge trash pits require heavy equipment like bulldozers and dump trucks to continually move and level out all the garbage.

1-3Y: Skills Card

Reader: _____ Room: _____

"What was this book mainly about? How do you know?"

1Y	Listen to and remember the sentence pattern in Yellow books. Use the pattern and pictures to read the rest of the book.

2Y	Point to each word as I read. Use the spaces to separate words.
	Try again if what I say doesn't match the number of words.

3Y	Make the sound of the first letter of the new word on the page, check the picture, then say something that matches both.

I can get my mouth ready for:

b	c	d
f	g	h
j	k	l
m	n	p
r	s	t
v	w	z